EXTINCT SPECIES

EXTINCT REPTILES AND AMPHIBIANS

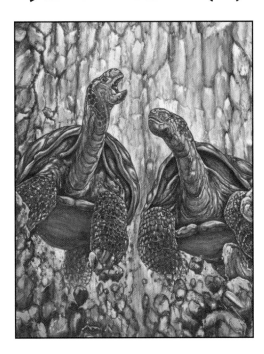

**First published in 2002 by
Grolier Educational
Sherman Turnpike
Danbury, Connecticut 06816**
© Quartz Editions 2002

Library of Congress Cataloging-in-Publication Data
Extinct species.

    p. cm.

  Contents: v. 1. Why extinction occurs - - v. 2. Prehistoric animal life - - v. 3. Fossil
hunting - - v. 4. Extinct mammals - - v. 5. Extinct birds - - v. 6 Extinct underwater life - -
v. 7. Extinct reptiles and amphibians - - v. 8. Extinct invertebrates and plants - - v. 9.
Hominids - - v. 10. Atlas of extinction.

  Summary: Examines extinct species, including prehistoric man, and discusses why
extinction happens, as well as how information is gathered on species that existed
before humans evolved.

ISBN 0-7172-5564-6 (set) - - ISBN 0-7172-5565-4 (v. 1) - - ISBN 0-7172-5566-2 (v. 2)
- - ISBN 0-7172-5567-0 (v. 3) - - ISBN 0-7172-5568-9 (v. 4) - - ISBN 0-7172-5569-7 (v.
5) - - ISBN 0-7172-5570-0 (v. 6) - - ISBN 0-7172-5571-9 (v. 7) - - ISBN 0-7172-5572-7
(v. 8) - - ISBN 0-7172-5573-5 (v. 9) - - ISBN 0-7172-5574-3 (v. 10)

  1. Extinction (Biology) - - Juvenile literature. 2. Extinct animals - - Juvenile literature.
[1. Extinction (Biology) 2. Extinct animals.] I. Grolier Educational.

  QH78 .E88 2002
  578.68 - - dc21   2001055702

**Produced by Quartz Editions
Premier House
112 Station Road
Edgware HA8 7BJ
UK**

EDITORIAL DIRECTOR: Tamara Green
CREATIVE DIRECTOR: Marilyn Franks
PRINCIPAL ILLUSTRATOR: Neil Lloyd
CONTRIBUTING ILLUSTRATORS: Tony Gibbons, Helen Jones
EDITORIAL CONTRIBUTOR: Graham Coleman

Reprographics by Mullis Morgan, London
Printed in Belgium by Proost

ACKNOWLEDGMENTS

The publishers wish to thank the following for supplying
photographic images for this volume.

Front & back cover t SPL/J.Baum & D.Angus

Page 1t SPL/J.Baum & D.Angus;
p3t SPL/J.Baum & D.Angus; p15t NHPA/A.N.T.;
p15br NHPA/E.Hanumantha Rao; p17t OSF/M.Fogden;
p17br MEPL; p22bl NHPA/G.Bernard;
p23br OSF/T.de Roy; p26bl NHPA/A.Bannister;
p27b OSF/F.Schneidermever; p31t BC/M.Fogden;
p34bl NHPA/M.Wendler; p34bc NHPA/M.Wendler;
p35t NHPA/B.Wood.

Abbreviations: Bruce Coleman (BC); Mary Evans Picture
Library (MEPL); Natural History Photographic Agency
(NHPA); Oxford Scientific Films (OSF); Science Photo Library
(SPL); bottom (b); center (c); left (l); right (r); top (t).

EXTINCT SPECIES

EXTINCT REPTILES AND AMPHIBIANS

GROLIER EDUCATIONAL

SHERMAN TURNPIKE, DANBURY, CONNECTICUT 06816

SNAKE-NECKED
This plant-eating dinosaur with a neck just like a snake was a typical sauropod from Jurassic times and makes an appearance on page 29.

UNDENIABLY UGLY
This creature was nicknamed Delilah as a joke when first unearthed in South Africa. What scientists know about its prehistoric existence is revealed on pages 18-19.

Contents

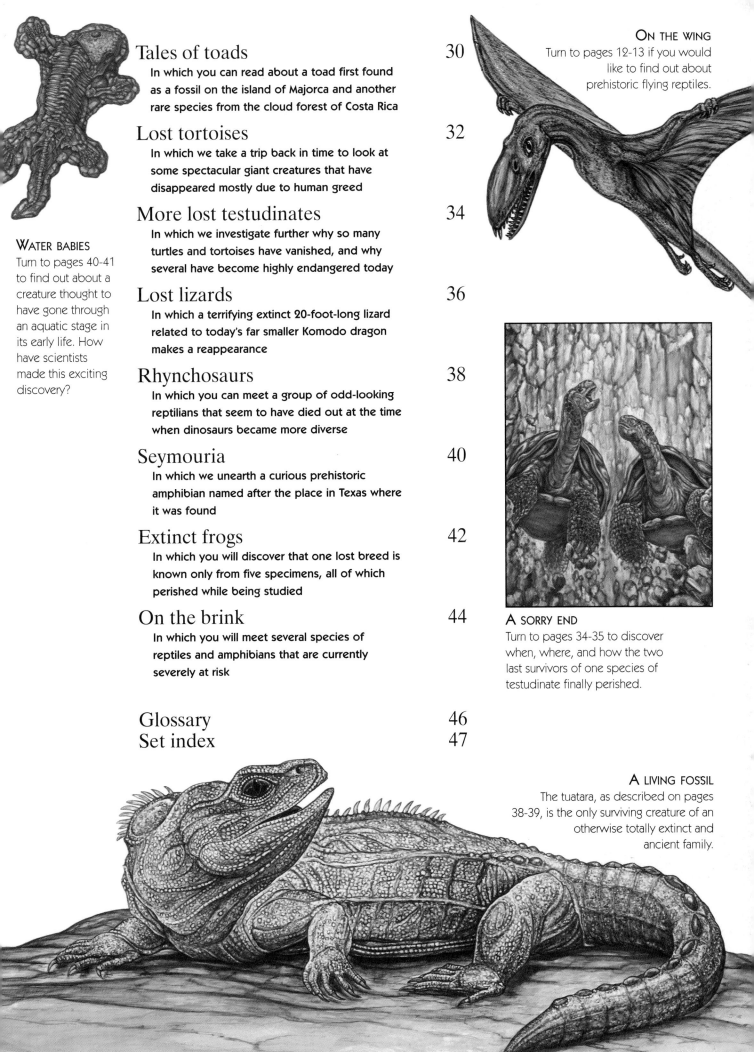

WATER BABIES
Turn to pages 40-41 to find out about a creature thought to have gone through an aquatic stage in its early life. How have scientists made this exciting discovery?

ON THE WING
Turn to pages 12-13 if you would like to find out about prehistoric flying reptiles.

A SORRY END
Turn to pages 34-35 to discover when, where, and how the two last survivors of one species of testudinate finally perished.

A LIVING FOSSIL
The tuatara, as described on pages 38-39, is the only surviving creature of an otherwise totally extinct and ancient family.

Introduction

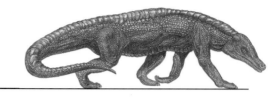

This bizarre-looking creature was a member of the thecodont family from Triassic times. In all, four different types of these reptiles evolved, but all became extinct about 180 million years ago.

COLD-BLOODED CREATURES?
Paleontologists are still trying to decide if the dinosaurs were definitely cold-blooded and so relied on external heat sources like the reptiles of today.

Many long-extinct reptiles were enormous. Way back in prehistoric times huge turtles – 13-foot-long *Archelon* (ARK-EL-ON) from Cretaceous times, for instance – swam in the warm oceans, their thick shells sure forms of protection against most marine predators. Enormous crocodilians like *Photosuchus* (FOH-TOH-SOOK-us), meanwhile, grew up to 50 feet in length. And many of the dinosaurs, which are, of course, classed as reptiles by zoologists, grew to be, as far as we know, among the largest creatures ever to have existed on our planet.

You are about to become acquainted with some of the most extraordinary extinct and endangered reptiles the world has ever known – snakes, geckoes, and skinks among them – and will meet, too, some fascinating amphibians. But why have so many of these creatures vanished from the planet?

BODY TALK
Why might some early reptiles, like the one *above*, have sported strange structures on their backs? Were they purely decorative, or did they have a definite purpose?

GIANT LIZARD
Our distant ancestors were no doubt terrified by this enormous lizard but are thought to have hunted it for its flesh.

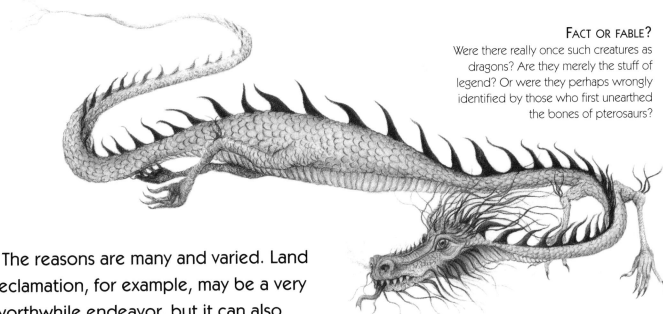

FACT OR FABLE?
Were there really once such creatures as dragons? Are they merely the stuff of legend? Or were they perhaps wrongly identified by those who first unearthed the bones of pterosaurs?

The reasons are many and varied. Land reclamation, for example, may be a very worthwhile endeavor, but it can also cause the demise of rare species. The Palestinian painted frog, for instance, was a scarce amphibian that completely disappeared when swamps by the shores of Lake Hula on the Israel-Syria border came to be drained. The Vegas Valley leopard frog of Nevada, meanwhile, is no longer to be seen in North America. The waters in which it had formerly thrived were diverted for human use, and larger bullfrogs only too readily gobbled up those few that remained.

Conservationists are eager to talk with developers so that ways can be found to preserve the natural habitats of endangered reptiles and amphibians before it is too late and certain species are lost forever. We have to face up to the fact that many simply fail to thrive in captivity.

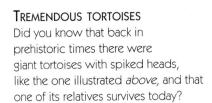

TREMENDOUS TORTOISES
Did you know that back in prehistoric times there were giant tortoises with spiked heads, like the one illustrated *above*, and that one of its relatives survives today?

GONE BUT NOT FORGOTTEN
The Palestinian painted frog, so-called because of its distinctive blotchy markings that look just like blobs of paint, disappeared when its Middle Eastern habitat was drained for agricultural use.

7

REPTILE OR NOT?

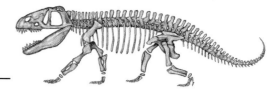

It is no easy matter for paleontologists to distinguish the fossilized remains of a prehistoric reptile from those of an amphibian. But there are certain clues they can look for. Read on and find out the main differences between present-day reptiles and amphibians, too.

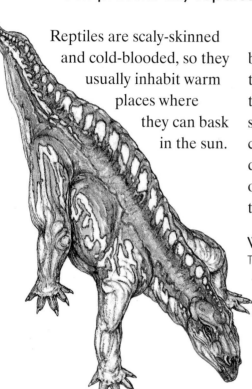

Reptiles are scaly-skinned and cold-blooded, so they usually inhabit warm places where they can bask in the sun.

Amphibians are also cold-blooded but spend only part of the time on land. They also like the water, where they lay their soft, jelly-covered eggs in large clusters, and generally have damp skin. Reptiles, on the other hand, will usually lay their hard-shelled eggs on land.

WARMING UP
The structure along the back of *Lotosaurus* (LOH-TOH-<u>SOR</u>-US), *left*, may have been used as a sort of solar panel to help keep this cold-blooded, plant-eating reptile warm.

RED HUNTER
A large reptile with a 3-foot-long head, *Erythrosuchus* (ER-ITH-ROH-<u>SOOK</u>-US), whose skeleton is shown *above*, lived mostly on land and was one of the most successful hunters of Early Triassic times. It was unearthed in South Africa and has a name meaning "red crocodile."

DISTANT ORIGINS
Early amphibians, such as *Ichthyostega* (<u>IK</u>-THEE-OST-<u>AY</u>-GAH), are thought to have evolved from fish and first appeared on the planet in Devonian times, about 3.7 million years ago. Some early amphibians probably even had scales and would have walked with an awkward gait on land, but swam confidently in the water.

FIRST CROCODILE
The reptile shown *right* was given its name, *Protosuchus* (<u>PROH</u>-TOH-<u>SOOK</u>-US), meaning "first crocodile," by the American fossil-hunter Barnum Brown. Note the row of plating along its back.

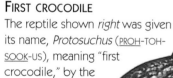

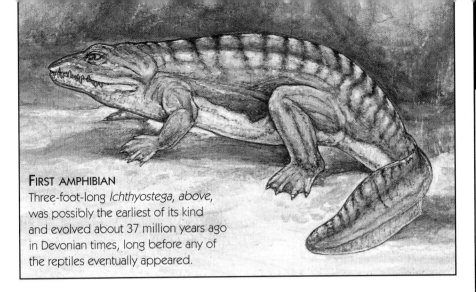

FIRST AMPHIBIAN
Three-foot-long *Ichthyostega, above,*
was possibly the earliest of its kind
and evolved about 37 million years ago
in Devonian times, long before any of
the reptiles eventually appeared.

Paleontologists think that the first shelled eggs were laid on land during Carboniferous times. By then a so-called amniotic egg had evolved. Inside its thinly shelled structure the developing young was protected by a bag of fluid, known as the amnion, while a yolk provided nourishment for the embryo before it hatched. Evolving reptiles could now safely lay their eggs on land.

During Early Permian times, when there were extremes of climate, both amphibians and reptiles lived mainly in tropical zones. The reptiles thrived and diversified over many millions of years, some evolving to become huge. Today we tend to think of amphibians as small, but back in time there were sturdy amphibians that were by no means the size of later, gigantic dinosaurs but still 5 feet or more in length – *Eryops* (ER-EE-OPS), for example.

At the end of Triassic times, when a mass extinction occurred, many amphibians seem to have been wiped out, and new, smaller species evolved. But certain reptiles – the dinosaurs – continued to evolve to even larger proportions.

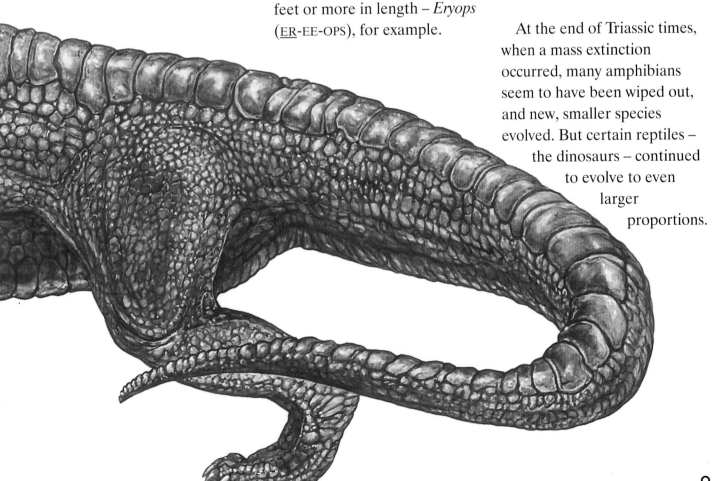

GLIDING LIZARDS

Fossils show that millions of years ago some reptiles had winglike flaps that helped them glide. They could not actually fly but used these membranes for making short excursions through the trees. One creature with similar aerial skills survives today.

In the tropical rain forests of southern India, the Philippines, and Borneo, when it is not raining and when the wind is low, a gliding lizard can sometimes be spotted as it leaps from branch to branch or descends to the ground. This species is known by the scientific name *Draco volans*, which means "flying dragon," and remains show it has ancestors that got around in a similar way long before pterosaurs (true flying reptiles) or birds first evolved.

From six fossils of the 12-inch-long lizard known as *Coelosauravus* (SOH-EL-OH-SOR-RAH-VUS) unearthed in Germany in 1910 by a miner, for instance, scientists can tell it could glide. At first, however, the German paleontologist Otto Jaekel thought its unusual wing bones were the remains of a fish that over millions of years had become fossilized on top of the lizard. He was wrong, however, and we now know they were not even extensions of its ribs but hollow bones that had evolved to support flight membranes or wings that could be folded like oriental fans when not in use.

Coelosauravus did not have feathers or powerful wing muscles like birds. But when a scale model was made of it and then tested, it proved to be an excellent glider over a distance of 40 feet.

Some paleontologists even think there were gliding lizards capable of propelling themselves along for up to 200 feet. No one is sure, however, whether they used such skills to catch insects because *Draco volans*, the modern equivalent, seems to have a sit-and-wait policy and does not spring in search of prey. Instead, it waits for a victim's approach and then snaps up its meal.

Other extinct winged lizards include *Icarosaurus* (IK-A-ROH-SOR-US), named after the god of Greek mythology who made wax wings so that he could fly, and *Kuehnosaurus* (KOO-EN-OH-SOR-US), both about 26 inches in length, with thin, longer back limbs and dating from Triassic times.

Another tiny prehistoric glider was *Longisquama* (LONG-IS-KWAH-MAH), which measured only 5 inches in length, and which had a row of long plumes rising from its back.

Paleontologists do not all agree about the function of these plumes. Some think they were used to control temperature; others, that they were there to attract a mate, or that they could be relied on to cushion a fall when gliding.

GREAT ESCAPES

Winged lizards would also no doubt glide in the attempt to get themselves out of trouble if a predator suddenly approached. Many of the smaller, meat-eating dinosaurs of that era certainly could have made short work of them.

Some scientists think that when some wingless lizards fled from predators, they sometimes ran so fast that they became airborne automatically for a short distance.

It is equally possible that the quest for safety drove some prehistoric gliding reptiles to develop longer necks and true wings, and then to take more confidently to the air.

Indeed, true flying reptiles, the pterosaurs, may have evolved from gliding lizards. In fact, alongside the remains of *Longisquama*, found in Kirgizstan, Central Asia, in 1970, were imprints of the skeleton of creature known as *Podopteryx* (POD-OPT-ER-IKS), meaning "foot-wing." It was clear that its wing membranes were attached not to elongated ribs but to its front limbs, just as they were to be in the far larger pterosaurs you can read about on pages 12-13 of this book.

Fact file

- One species of gliding lizard has survived to this day, probably due to being able to change color and camouflage itself to escape predators. It is the so-called flying dragon of the jungles of Southeast Asia.

- The gliding lizards would sometimes scamper along branches with their wing membranes tucked away, so they did nor become entangled in the forest vegetation.

- Winged lizards probably formed part of the diet of smaller meat-eating dinosaurs throughout Triassic, Jurassic, and Cretaceous times, and so would have been constantly vulnerable.

- Most gliding lizards had lengthy tails which helped them balance.

GREAT MOVERS
The two prehistoric lizards in the illustration *left* are shown with their wing flaps extended, enabling them to move through the air just like a modern glider plane. Note the bones supporting their wing flaps, and that, unlike birds, they had four limbs.

FLYING REPTILES

When a very strange fossil was unearthed in Germany in the mid-18th century, no one was sure what it was. Some thought it was a type of bat; others, a waterfowl. It was, however, an entirely different life form – a *pterosaur* (TER-OH-SOR), or ancient reptile that could fly.

Attached to their forelimbs were membranes that could be flexed to an umbrella shape. There was now greater air pressure below the membranes than above them, so that they had liftoff. Light, hollow bones meant they did not come down to Earth with a bump.

Pterosaurs first evolved in Triassic times; so while dinosaurs walked on the ground and sometimes paddled in the sea, these flying reptiles flew high above them. Some were huge. The remains of Cretaceous *Quetzalcoatlus* (KWET-ZAL-COHT-LUS), for example, discovered in 1971 in Texas, show a wingspan of 39 feet, the size of a modern light aircraft. However, it only weighed about 190 pounds.

INSECT-CATCHER
Long-tailed and with a wing span of around 2 feet, *Peteinosaurus* (PET-EYE-NOH-SOR-US) had large front teeth in front of smaller, pointed ones – which suggests it caught insects.

Airplanes have engines, and birds have feathers. The pterosaurs had neither, though. So how did these creatures get airborne? They would usually launch themselves from trees and take advantage of air currents to help them rise. Then they would use their muscles to pull their forelimbs up and down in a flapping motion.

Scientists have even calculated the speed at which they flew. A pterosaur with a wingspan of about 30 feet, for example, could probably fly at the phenomenal rate of 24 feet per second.

EARLY FIND
One of the first pterosaurs to evolve, *Preondactylus* (PRAY-ON-DAKT-EE-LUS), was discovered in northern Italy. It had a wing span of just 18 inches.

JURASSIC FROG-JAW
With a name meaning "frog-jaw," *Batrachognathus* (BAT-RAH-KOG-NARTH-US) had teeth that were like pegs and probably lived on a diet of insects. Its wingspan extended to about 1.7 feet, but so far no complete skeleton has been found.

12

Some pterosaur fossil finds have yielded perfectly preserved stomach contents, so that paleontologists know these flying reptiles were fish-eaters. Rows of sharp teeth were ideal for grabbing hold of slippery marine life, and a small pouch of skin on the lower jaw may have been used to store the catch for later. Some pterosaurs, however, had hundreds of very thin, fine teeth, completely unsuited to biting but useful for filtering out any small creatures they scooped up from the water. The short, blunt teeth of some pterosaurs, meanwhile, were perfect for mashing up food into digestible pieces.

Paleontologists have assumed pterosaurs laid eggs, though no one has yet found one. Fossilized shells found near their remains possibly belonged to these flying reptiles. Some of them may have congregated in hatching colonies, leaving all the eggs in the care of one or two adults. Once safely hatched following incubation in the sun, the baby pterosaurs were then probably fed with half-digested food and guarded against predators until they could fend for themselves.

Although they flew well, pterosaurs were not related in any way to birds, which – perhaps surprisingly – have a link with the dinosaurs.

Fact file

● Some pterosaurs may have hung upside down from a branch to sleep, enclosing themselves in their wing membranes so that they were compact, just like a giant pod.

● Some scientists think pterosaurs may sometimes have provided screeched warnings for any small dinosaur about to become the victim of a giant meat-eater.

● Some pterosaurs had short tails; some, far longer ones.

● Pterosaurs became extinct, along with the dinosaurs, at the end of Cretaceous times, about 65 million years ago. During their existence many new types of pterosaur evolved, while others seem to have died out.

A MOUTHFUL OF BRISTLES
Found in Argentina, *Pterodaustro* (TERR-OH-DOW-STROH) had a wing span of 4.3 feet, very long, upwardly bent jaws, and strange teeth that were like the bristles of a brush – ideal for sifting out small fish.

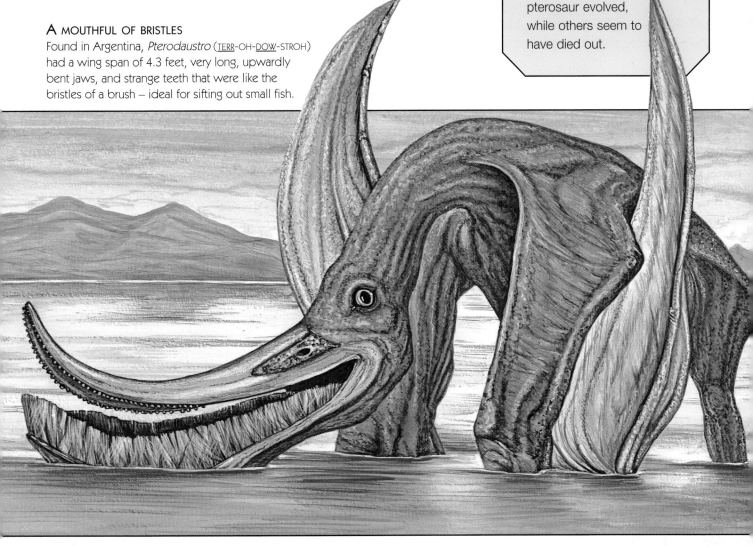

VANISHING CROCODILES

It is just as well that no humans yet existed when a crocodilian known as *Sarchosuchus imperator* (SAR-KOH-SOOK-US IMP-ERR-AH-TOR) roamed our planet. Able to down about one-fifth of its body weight at a time, it could easily have eaten you and a friend for breakfast.

Longer than a bus and with the most deadly jaws, *Sarchosuchus imperator* was discovered in the Teneré Desert of Niger, Africa, back in 1964. However, only a few isolated bones belonging to this prehistoric river monster were found.

TEN-TON PREDATOR
As this illustration shows, *Sarchosuchus* often came out of the water to seek its prey. Few animals of the time could have withstood its attack.

But in the year 2000 as many as 12 specimens were unearthed by a team of paleontologists led by Professor Paul Soreno of Chicago University. It was a tricky expedition, and armed guards were required because of serious political instability in the region.

These crocodilians were the principal predators of Cretaceous times. Using their razor-sharp teeth, they had no hesitation in attacking far bigger creatures on the shore and then dragging the victims underwater.

Even the very largest of the dinosaurs living in what is now Africa were at risk when *Sarchosuchus* was on the prowl.

Early turtles, in spite of their hard shells, were vulnerable. *Sarchosuchus* would simply flip them over so that their soft underbellies were exposed to the predator's scything teeth.

SUPERCROC
Sarchosuchus took a long time to grow and did not reach full adult size until around the age of 50, by which time it would have weighed many tons. Its lifespan is thought to have extended to 90 years.

ONE OF THE FAMILY
Sarchosuchus was a distant cousin of the modern endangered Australian species of crocodile shown *above*, and the largest crocodilian ever known.

Dubbed "supercroc" by those who have studied its anatomy, *Sarchosuchus* had some extraordinary features. Its eyes, for instance, could be rotated upward, so that even while submerged, it could look for any unsuspecting prey coming to the water's edge to drink. Then there would have been mayhem as *Sarchosuchus* grappled with its victim using its fearsome, elongated snout to inflict horrific wounds. Its quarry, meanwhile, no doubt gave out loud shrieks of terror, warning any others of its kind to steer clear.

ON SWAMPY GROUND

Cretaceous swamplands were damp, gloomy places; and in parts, forests of high cypresses, ginkgoes, and seed-ferns blotted out the light. But the swamps provided a lush habitat for semi-aquatic creatures such as *Sarchosuchus*.

IN DECLINE
The endangered crocodilian, *right* – *Gavialis gangeticus* (GAV-EE-AH-LIS GANJ-ET-IK-US) – has even longer jaws than *Sarchosuchus* did but is smaller in length. It has been overhunted for its skin.

THE FAMILY LINE

How, though, did crocodilians first evolve? In Early Triassic times (about 250 million years ago) a group of creatures known as archosaurs (ARK-OH-SORS) branched out into two main groups. One of these groups led to the dinosaurs and birds; the other, to the crocodilians.

One difference between these two groups of archosaurs lay in their ankles. Crocodilians had a complex joint that allowed some rotation of the feet, but dinosaurs had an ankle joint more like a hinge, so that movement was mostly restricted to upward and downward flapping. You can read more about archosaurs in the volume on *Prehistoric Animal Life* that is part of this set.

STRANGE BUT TRUE

It may seem odd, but certain crocodile ancestors, such as *Terrestrisuchus* (TER-EST-REE-SOOK-US) from the Late Triassic and unearthed in Wales, looked very unlike the crocodiles we know today and even seem to have had such long hind limbs that they may have been bipedal – that is, they may have walked on two legs only. What classifies them as crocodilian, however, is their basic bone structure.

ANDRIAS SCHEUCHZERI

The fossilized bones of this creature once sparked a fierce scientific debate. Were they proof humans had perished in a prehistoric flood that engulfed the world? Or were they the remains of one of the most ancient creatures ever to have lived on our planet?

In 1725 Swiss naturalist Johann Jakob Scheuchzer examined some curious remains dug up in Germany.

EARLY HABITATS
The first remains of an ancient salamander like the one *below* were discovered in Germany, but the best finds have been made more recently in Asia.

They clearly belonged to a vertebrate, which Scheuchzer named *Homo diluvii testis* (HO-MOH DIL-<u>OO</u>-VEE-EE <u>TEST</u>-IS), meaning "man who witnessed the deluge," since he was convinced they must have been the remains of an early human being who had been a victim of the biblical flood. Not everyone was so sure, however.

Other scientists expressed grave doubts; but it was not until several years later, in 1811, that the French scientist Georges Cuvier got round to cleaning the remains and reexamining them. What he now proclaimed shook the world. This was no human, but a giant species of salamander!

RENAMED FOSSIL
In recognition of the first man to examine the fossil, however, the creature was renamed *Andrias scheuchzeri* (<u>AN</u>-DREE-AS <u>SKOYK</u>-ZAIR-EE). Since then fossils of many giant salamanders have been found in Europe, Asia, and North America, showing they were once very common.

A MODERN RELATIVE

The presentday yellow and black European fire salamander in the photograph *above* is remarkably similar to its ancestor, *Andrias scheuchzeri*, illustrated on page 16.

Salamanders are extremely ancient creatures and developed from the first vertebrates to crawl onto land from the seas some 350 million years ago. We also know from their fossils that these ancient salamanders must have been very similar in appearance to their modern relatives.

Salamanders, like frogs, are classed as amphibians but are often mistaken for lizards, which are reptiles. There are some important differences, though. A salamander's skin is moist, it does not have claws on its toes, and it is without an ear hole of any kind. In fact, it cannot hear sounds through the air at all, although it does feel some vibrations through its bones. Instead, salamanders rely wholly on their senses of smell and taste to tell if a predator is approaching or if perhaps a potential meal is near at hand.

With its lidless eyes, stumpy legs, and bumpy head, *Andrias scheuchzeri* was certainly not an attractive creature.

It could breathe both on land and when it was underwater, where it spent most of its time. The blotchy, bumpy skin around its head consisted of blood vessels that allowed it to absorb oxygen through its skin so that it could stay underwater for long periods of time.

FEEDING TIME

Giant salamanders were not very active creatures; and with a low rate of metabolism, they were able to go without food for long periods, too. When *Andrias Scheuchzeri* did need food, however, it had little trouble finding any. With its wide mouth and strong jaws, it could quickly catch and devour its prey, feeding mainly on fish, frogs, and small reptiles, as well as insect snacks.

It was also fortunate in being far too large to be caught by most of the predators of its era – one of the reasons why such giant salamanders survived on this planet for so many millions of years.

Fact file

● The oldest salamander fossils ever found were dug up in China in 1997. They date from 150 million years ago, during Jurassic times. They are thought to have died when a volcano erupted, and ash poured down on the pond in which the creatures were living. Over 500 individual remains were found.

● There are around 300 different species of salamander living today. This may sound like a large figure, but it is in fact far fewer than existed back in prehistoric times.

● Today's giant salamanders can grow up to 5 feet in length and are known to have lived for as long as 55 years.

● Contrary to myth, salamanders cannot survive in fire.

MISTAKEN IDENTITY

Scheuchzer wrongly believed the fossil he examined was part of a man who had perished in the biblical flood, depicted in the painting shown *below*.

17

PAREIASAURS

Approximately 250 million years after she walked alive on our planet back in Permian times, a mighty *Pareiasaurus* (PA-REYE-A-SOR-US) was nicknamed Delilah, after the biblical character, by the scientists who unearthed her fossilized skeleton in South Africa.

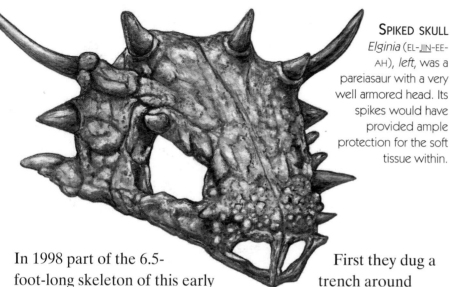

SPIKED SKULL
Elginia (EL-JIN-EE-AH), *left*, was a pareiasaur with a very well armored head. Its spikes would have provided ample protection for the soft tissue within.

In 1998 part of the 6.5-foot-long skeleton of this early reptile became exposed on a mountain side. It was found in a crouching position, and its many interlocking plates were still covering its back. As possibly the best preserved specimen of this species, it was an incredible find. However there was one major problem. How could the team excavate it speedily while keeping it intact?

First they dug a trench around Delilah, and then they encased her in plaster of Paris to protect her skeletal remains. Unfortunately, however, no craft could be found locally to provide an adequate airlift.

There was nothing else to do. The team, assisted by several tough young men from nearby farms, had to combine forces and lift what they estimated to be a 1,543-pound creature. It took much huffing and puffing.

A FITTING NAME?

Delilah, as you might have guessed, was given her name with tongue in cheek. After all, she was hardly as beautiful as her namesake, who betrayed Samson in the well known Bible story! Indeed, reconstructions, like the one in the illustration *far right*, show *Pareiasaurus* had a formidable appearance. Its ugly, bulky body was covered with a knobby outer coating formed from bony protuberances, and the head was also protected in this way.

In fact, its eyes were hardly visible among all those bumps of bone and seemed embedded in the uneven surface. It also had very broad limbs and stocky legs to support its powerful frame.

UNTIMELY END

Living long before the dinosaurs had evolved, *Pareiasaurus* met its demise during the mass extinction that seems to have occurred at the end of Permian times, about 250 million years ago. It has even been estimated that about 95% of all species existing then completely disappeared. No one is entirely sure why this happened. Some experts think the climate may have changed dramatically so that it could no longer support life as it was then.

PAREIASAURUS IN PROFILE
The fossil, *left*, is typical of the skulls of *Pareiasaurus* discovered in South Africa. Note its very regular teeth and the nodules that rise from the surface of the bone.

Others contend there was a marked change in sea level, that the lava and ash from extensive volcanic eruptions may have devastated both flora and fauna, or that an asteroid hit Earth. Whatever the cause, only a few species survived, and *Pareiasaurus* does not seem to have been one of them.

Relatives of *Pareiasaurus* included *Scutosaurus* (<u>SKUT</u>-OH-<u>SOR</u>-US), a massive plant-eater inhabiting what is now Russia, and *Bradysaurus* (<u>BRAY</u>-DEE-<u>SOR</u>-US) from South Africa.

In both regions they lived alongside creatures known as dinocephalians (<u>DEYE</u>-NOH-SEF-<u>AYL</u>-EE-ANZ), which were similar in appearance, but which had different needs from each other. The pareiasaurs are thought to have preferred warm lowlands as a habitat, while the dinocephalians liked the forested uplands. Fossil evidence also shows that the dinocephalians were probably more numerous and died out some time before the pareiasaurs disappeared.

Fact file

- The skeleton of a young *Pareiasaurus*, complete with skull, was found in the region of Kotelnich, Russia. Others of its family group have been unearthed in Brazil.

- Some scientists believe pareiasaurs were semiaquatic, occasionally entering the water, and that they possibly evolved into turtles.

- Scientists have found fairly complete skeletal remains of various species of pareiasaurs undisturbed by the action of any predators.

- Pareiasaurs are classed as anapsids, which means they were reptiles characterized by the absence of any skull openings behind their eyes.

WHAT A BRUTE!

Pareiasaurus, seen *right* in an artist's impression, could not have been more frightening in appearance. It measured almost 10 feet in length and had the roughest, knobby body covering you can imagine. Its peglike teeth, however, were small and even in size.

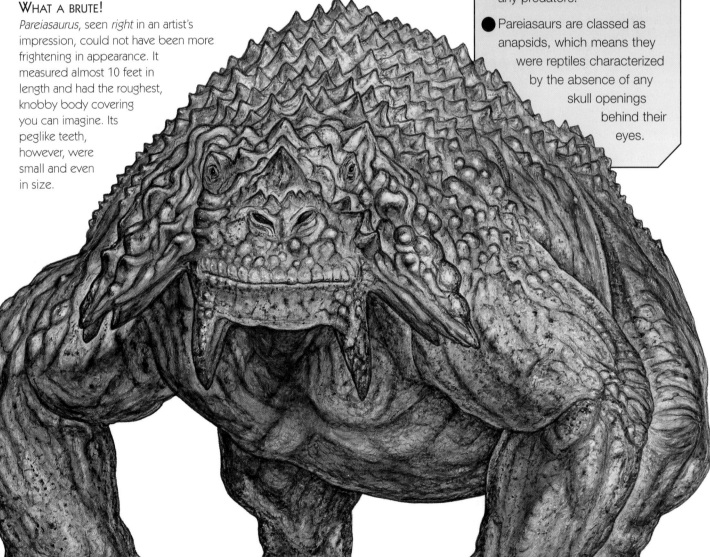

PELYCOSAURS

Although they would have seemed clumsy when walking because of their sprawling legs and the large, upright structures on their backs, these creatures were very resourceful reptiles.

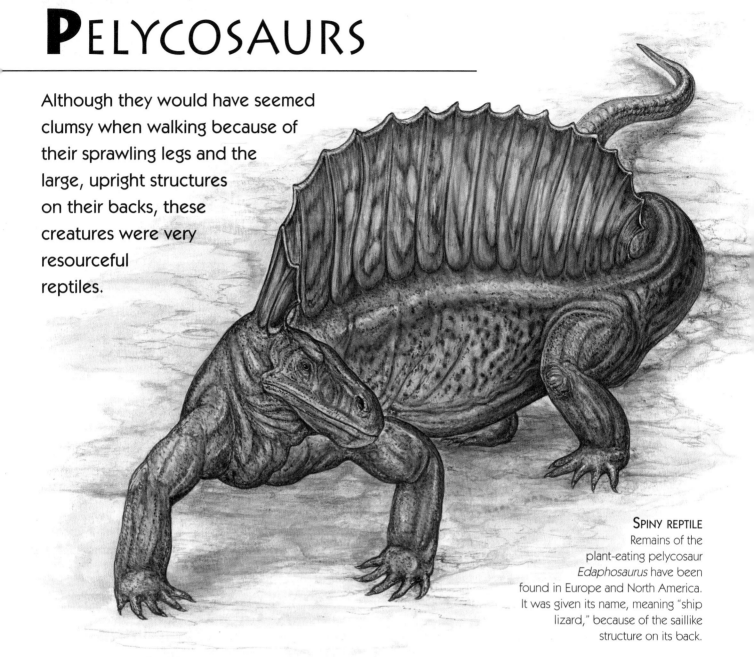

SPINY REPTILE
Remains of the plant-eating pelycosaur *Edaphosaurus* have been found in Europe and North America. It was given its name, meaning "ship lizard," because of the saillike structure on its back.

Pelycosaurs (<u>PEL</u>-EE-KOH-SORS) were prehistoric reptiles inhabiting swampy areas during Permian times, long before dinosaurs first appeared on our planet. The earliest were small, lizardlike creatures, but over time they evolved into a variety of larger animals. Some ate fish, crustaceans, and a variety of small animals, while others were strictly plant-eating. But whatever their favored diet, one thing many pelycosaurs had in common were the spines they sported on their backs.

Scientists believe these spines may have helped the pelycosaurs regulate their body temperature. Reptiles do not have hair or feathers and so find it difficult to keep themselves warm. These upright, skin-covered structures may even have had a dual purpose. The surface area of the spines may have acted like a solar panel, absorbing heat on colder days, and may also have helped shield a pelycosaur from direct sunlight if it became too hot at midday.

BULKY BODY

Edaphosaurus (<u>E</u>-DAFF-OH-<u>SOR</u>-US), a typical pelycosaur, grew up to 10 feet in length and had strong legs, a long tail, and a small head. Rows of fossilized teeth, well suited to grinding rather than cutting through flesh, show that it was a herbivore. *Dimetrodon* (DEYE-<u>MET</u>-ROH-<u>DON</u>), another pelycosaur, was similar in appearance to *Edaphosaurus*; but its fossilized remains clearly show it had the sharp teeth typical of a meat-eater.

A pelycosaur could move the spiny structure on its back so that heat would pass down it and warm up its body. The spines were covered by skin although, as with most remains of prehistoric animals, only the bones survive.

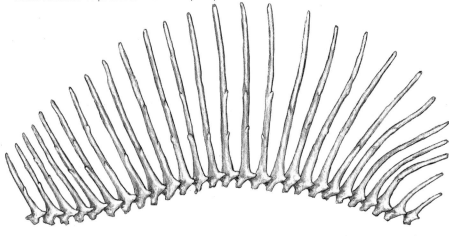

Fact file

- Although they are classed as reptiles, which are cold-blooded creatures, pelycosaurs were ancestors of the warm-blooded mammals, which produce their body heat from the inside. Mammals did not evolve until the end of Permian times.

- Pelycosaurs have a name meaning "basin lizard." They became extinct before the start of Triassic times, when the dinosaurs first evolved.

- The world's oldest reptile egg was found in Texas. It was two and a half inches long and so probably belonged to a large reptile such as *Dimetrodon* or *Edaphosaurus*.

- Some scientists think the sails of pelycosaurs were used for sexual display.

Indeed, *Edaphosaurus* may well have been a likely target for a hungry meat-eating pelycosaur such as *Dimetrodon*. However, it is likely to have remained within its herd whenever such a predator was on the prowl.

Dimetrodon grew up to 11 feet in length, and experts estimate it would have weighed around 550 pounds. An even larger pelycosaur, however, was *Cotylorhyncus* (KOT-EE-LOH-RIN-KUS) which, taking into account its very long tail, could grow to 13 feet in length.

HIGH AND MIGHTY
A *Dimetrodon's* spined sail was higher toward the center and covered with skin, giving it a very majestic appearance.

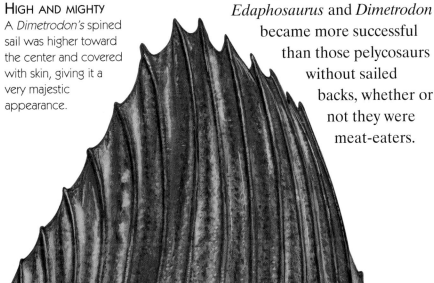

But as one of the more primitive pelycosaurs, *Cotylorhyncus* did not have a sail; nor did 5-foot-long *Varanosaurus* (VA-RAN-OH-SOR-US), unearthed in Texas and Oklahoma, which resembled a monitor lizard.

Having a sail, though, would have proved an advantage in the long run, since control over body temperature would have allowed the pelycosaurs to move around more freely. Since weather conditions changed a lot during Permian times, pelycosaurs such as *Edaphosaurus* and *Dimetrodon* became more successful than those pelycosaurs without sailed backs, whether or not they were meat-eaters.

It seems that sail-backed reptiles were well equipped to survive away from the swamps when conditions grew drier.

END OF AN ERA
Be that as it may, no pelycosaur survived beyond the end of Permian times, having first evolved 340 million years earlier. Along with many other animals and plants, the pelyocsaurs died out at the time of the greatest mass extinction our planet has ever known. It occurred at the end of a huge span of time that scientists refer to as the Paleozoic, a term derived from the ancient Greek and meaning "of very early organisms."

DID DRAGONS EVER EXIST?

The dragons that feature in legends of old may not be mere figments of the imagination. Instead, it has been suggested they may perhaps have been a primitive attempt to explain the origin of pterosaur remains that were dug up entirely by chance.

The folklore of many countries of the world includes accounts of amazing dragons that could fly through the skies and that sometimes breathed fire. On the whole, people were terrified of them. But they were sometimes slain by such national heroes as St. George, who became patron saint of England.

Other stories, meanwhile, are more fanciful. The German composer Richard Wagner, for example, wrote the music for an opera, *Siegfried*, which tells of a feared dragon called Fafnir that lived in a cave, and whose task was to guard a hoard of valuable treasure.

In most such accounts dragons, whether large or small, are portrayed as looking like large lizards, with scaly skin, clawed feet, and flapping wings. In fact, the dragons featured in both western and oriental literature definitely bear a strong resemblance to the reconstructions of pterosaur remains unearthed by paleontologists and now on display in many of the world's natural history museums.

ANOTHER LOOKALIKE
The extinct ring-tailed iguana, *left*, was also very dragonlike in appearance, with its very long body and ridged back, and may have been mistaken for one at times. It was native to Jamaica, in the West Indies, but has not been seen there since 1968.

JUST AN ILLUSION
Traditionally, dragons such as the one *above* are said to breathe fire. In this respect the Komodo dragon is true to its given name because the illusion created by its golden flicking tongue certainly gives the impression it is spouting fire from its mouth and nostrils.

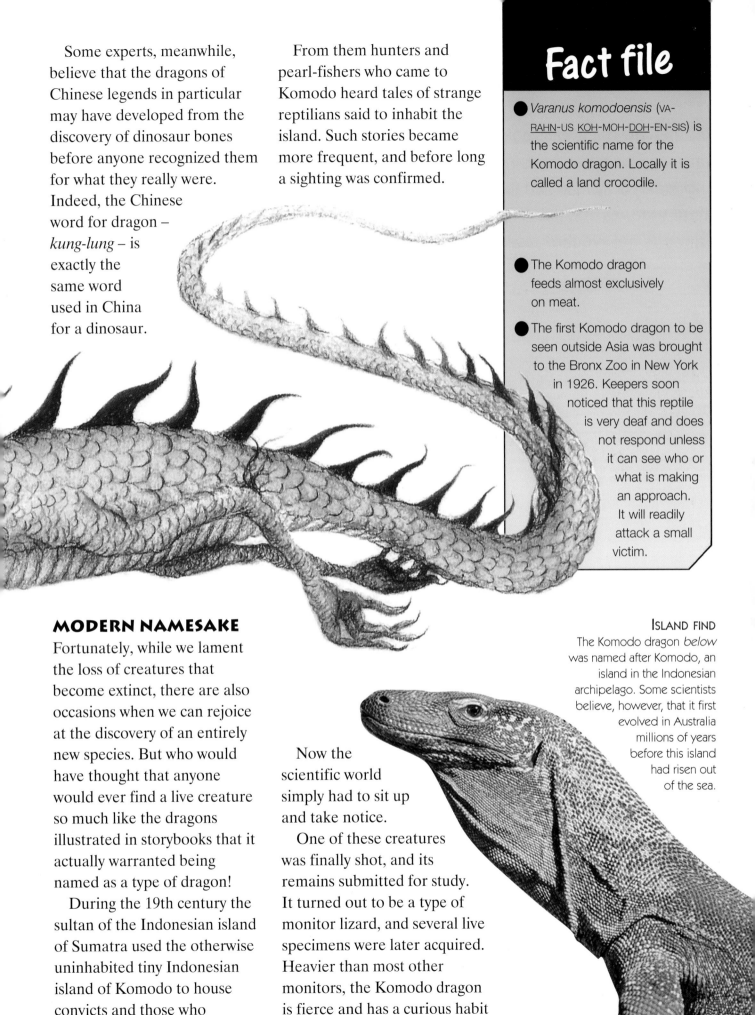

Some experts, meanwhile, believe that the dragons of Chinese legends in particular may have developed from the discovery of dinosaur bones before anyone recognized them for what they really were. Indeed, the Chinese word for dragon – *kung-lung* – is exactly the same word used in China for a dinosaur.

From them hunters and pearl-fishers who came to Komodo heard tales of strange reptilians said to inhabit the island. Such stories became more frequent, and before long a sighting was confirmed.

Fact file

● *Varanus komodoensis* (VA-RAHN-US KOH-MOH-DOH-EN-SIS) is the scientific name for the Komodo dragon. Locally it is called a land crocodile.

● The Komodo dragon feeds almost exclusively on meat.

● The first Komodo dragon to be seen outside Asia was brought to the Bronx Zoo in New York in 1926. Keepers soon noticed that this reptile is very deaf and does not respond unless it can see who or what is making an approach. It will readily attack a small victim.

MODERN NAMESAKE

Fortunately, while we lament the loss of creatures that become extinct, there are also occasions when we can rejoice at the discovery of an entirely new species. But who would have thought that anyone would ever find a live creature so much like the dragons illustrated in storybooks that it actually warranted being named as a type of dragon!

During the 19th century the sultan of the Indonesian island of Sumatra used the otherwise uninhabited tiny Indonesian island of Komodo to house convicts and those who opposed his regime.

Now the scientific world simply had to sit up and take notice.

One of these creatures was finally shot, and its remains submitted for study. It turned out to be a type of monitor lizard, and several live specimens were later acquired. Heavier than most other monitors, the Komodo dragon is fierce and has a curious habit of flicking its long tongue.

ISLAND FIND
The Komodo dragon *below* was named after Komodo, an island in the Indonesian archipelago. Some scientists believe, however, that it first evolved in Australia millions of years before this island had risen out of the sea.

THE DINOSAURS

Reptiles are defined as cold-blooded vertebrates with lungs and an outer covering of scales or plates that also lay eggs from which their young hatch. Most of these features apply to the dinosaurs, but some scientists believe they may have been warm-blooded.

NOISY BEAST

An adult *Parasaurolophus* (<u>PA</u>-RA-SOR-<u>ROL</u>-OH-FUS), seen drinking with one of its young from a pool in the illustration *above*, had an enormous tube projecting from the top of its head. Through this it could make booming noises to warn others in the herd about the approach of a predator.

The word dinosaur actually means "terrible reptile" and was given to this group of land animals by the great 19th-century British paleontologist Sir Richard Owen, who studied their fossilized remains. Their very name therefore suggests that, like most reptiles, they were probably ectothermic (the scientific term for cold-blooded.) However, an American paleontologist called Bob Bakker noted various points about the dinosaurs that suggested at least some of them may have been endothermic, or warm-blooded. Several factors drew him to this conclusion – among them, the dinosaurs' upright posture, which was like that of mammals and birds, and their active lifestyle. But not all scientists agreed, and so Bakker's theory led to a longstanding debate that continues today, even though the general consensus of opinion is that dinosaurs must have been ectothermic, with a body temperature that was controlled externally.

STILL A MYSTERY

Four-fingered hands and a very prominent nose horn were the main features of *Ceratosaurus* (<u>SER</u>-AT-OH-<u>SOR</u>-US), shown *left*. Its remains have been found in North America and Tanzania, Africa. Paleontologists remain perplexed about the function of the horn.

ON THE BACK OF IT

One of the extraordinary characteristics of the huge therapod dinosaur *Spinosaurus* (<u>SPEYE</u>-NOH-<u>SOR</u>-US) was the large crest that rose from its back. Most paleontologists think it was not purely ornamental but that it related in some way to temperature control.

Around the middle of Cretaceous times the temperature on Earth reached a level likely to have been higher than it has ever been since, and many paleontologists are now convinced this would have provided ideal conditions for reptiles and other creatures that were ectothermic. Certainly, the dinosaurs continued to thrive during the Cretaceous period. Mammals, which were endothermic, did not fare so well in such high temperatures, however; and so gigantic crocodiles and monstrous aquatic reptiles, such as the plesiosaurs and mosasaurs, became dominant in the warm seas.

Toward the end of Cretaceous times, however, the climate became generally cooler, due partly to alterations in the ocean currents. Slowly, more distinct seasons appeared, and winters grew much colder than before, with the result that some forms of plant life disappeared. Most scientists hold that dinosaurs became extinct at the end of Cretaceous times (the Cretaceous-Tertiary or KT boundary) due to asteroid impact. But some believe it was due to climatic change that may even have caused mostly male dinosaurs (or too many females) to hatch for them ever to mate in large numbers.

GETTING TO THE HEART OF THE MATTER

Paleontologists still cannot agree about the mechanism of a dinosaur's circulatory system. Some, such as *Diplodocus, below,* were so tall that it must have been difficult for the heart to pump sufficient blood all the way to the brain, particularly when their long necks were raised.

LOST SNAKES

The Round Island boa is believed to have been extinct since 1980. Another boa, meanwhile, the Madagascan variety, is severely endangered. First prize for length and girth must go, however, to the ancient giant boa, shown *right*.

ANCIENT STRANGLER
The boa *below* is now extinct, but this giant reptile was once native to Australia. It was greatly feared by the Aborigines because it was capable of killing a human through its stranglehold. Many folktales have grown up around it.

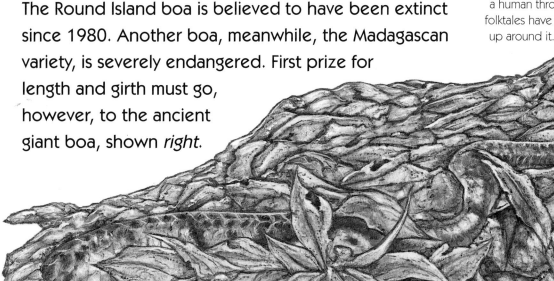

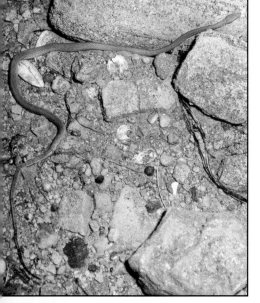

An enormously powerful snake, the giant boa would have been highly dangerous, killing its victims by wrapping its body around them and then tightening its grip until they suffocated. It may indeed be what was once thought to have been a mythical serpent featuring in the legends of the Australian Aborigine people.

Fossilized remains show that it grew up to 16.5 feet in length and that it was extremely chunky. Indeed, its central body seems to have been as wide as your chest. We do not know why this giant boa became extinct long ago, but scientists explain the extinction of several other snakes by human interference.

MASTER OF CAMOUFLAGE

It would have been difficult to spot the slithery Round Island boa, *left*, now effectively extinct, among the stones, gravel, and sandy soil that formed its habitat off the north coast of Mauritius in the Indian Ocean.

The boa from Round Island, near Mauritius, for example, of which only one or two may remain, lost its natural habitat when rabbits and goats were let loose into the wild on Round Island, only to deprive a large area of any sort of vegetation.

In the West Indies, meanwhile, snakes such as the Jamaican tree snake and the Martinique racer have disappeared due to hunting by humans and attack by the predatory mongoose in a few instances.

Sometimes snakes are treated extremely cruelly. In fact, they are skinned alive in some parts of the world because the quality of their skin is preserved that way. Then they are sold to the fashion trade. In Thailand they are also killed so people can drink their blood, which is thought to give the consumer increased vitality. They are caught for food in some places, too.

But why should we be concerned if some species of snakes, never popular creatures, become extinct?

After all, throughout history they have been a symbol of evil and death. The deadly king cobra is even known to have a bite that can kill humans in just a few minutes as its poison spreads through the body.

Snakes are, in fact, very important for controlling pest species, such as rodents and certain unpleasant insects. Indeed, in parts of the world where some types of snake have been entirely eradicated, such pests have become a serious danger, spreading potentially fatal diseases among the human population.

In the future it could also be that scientists may even find snakes have a number of valuable medicinal uses. Researchers at the University of Southern California, for example, suspect a protein they have found in the venom of the copperhead snake can be used to slow down the growth of a form of cancer. Interestingly, too, venom from the Brazilian arrowhead viper has been shown to assist in the lowering of human blood pressure.

If we do everything we can to save the world's snakes from extinction, it could be that, in turn, we will save humanity.

FAST DISAPPEARING
The San Francisco garter snake, *below*, declined in number after overgrown banks in which it hid by the side of inlets were cleared to improve the flow of water.

LONG-NECKED WONDERS

A number of prehistoric land and marine reptiles, particularly the sauropod dinosaurs and the plesiosaurs, had the most extraordinary necks. Why might they have become so elongated? And which extinct animal had the longest neck of all?

GOING FISHING
With such a lengthy neck, *Tanystropheus, below,* would have been able to use it much like a fishing rod to haul in the huge quantities of the marine life on which it fed.

A long neck was very practical for the sauropod dinosaurs of Jurassic times. It meant they could stretch right up to feed from the treetops in peace and quiet without competition from other, smaller herbivores. Since their necks were flexible, they could also swoop right down to the water's edge to quench their thirst. An upward bend in the joints that linked sturdy lower neck bones to the rest of the body shows that these towering creatures would have held their heads high but not entirely upright for most of the time. The vertebrae were very light, with an internal honeycomb structure, and that went a long way toward helping the sauropods move their necks more easily.

Scientists once thought the largest sauropod dinosaurs might have been aquatic creatures, using their long necks like snorkels to help them breathe. We now know, however, that they were definitely land-based, only occasionally going into the shallows to cool down.

But sauropod dinosaurs were not the only extinct creatures to have had very long necks. The animal depicted *above* and *far right,* for instance, is a *Tanystropheus* (<u>TAN</u>-IST-ROH-<u>FAY</u>-us), an offshoot of early lizards that lived by the coast in Europe during Triassic times, before the age of the sauropods. From fossil finds we know its eleven vertebrae were each 9 inches long, giving it a fantastic total neck length of over 12 feet.

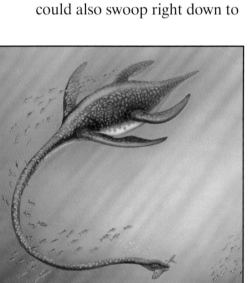

HALF AND HALF
The largest plesiosaur neck unearthed so far belonged to an *Elasmosaurus* (<u>EL</u>-AZ-MOH-<u>SOR</u>-us), meaning "ribbon reptile." Its neck alone measured 23 feet.

RECORD-BREAKER
A dinosaur from China with the name *Mamenchisaurus* (<u>MAM</u>-EN-KEE-<u>SOR</u>-us) is believed to have had the world's longest neck. From its partial remains scientists figure the whole animal was 89 feet long, and the neck alone a staggering 49 feet.

OH, MY, OH MY!
The *Omeisaurus* (OH-MEYE-<u>SOR</u>-US) in the illustration *right* was a typical sauropod dating from Jurassic times. Fossilized remains, found in China, show its whole body extended to 66 feet in length. As you can see, about half of this was neck.

Fact file

● Whenever the long-necked dinosaurs drank from a river or pool, they would have had to swing their necks down in an action resembling that of a present-day mechanical crane.

● *Giraffatian* (<u>JEER</u>-AF-<u>AT</u>-EE-AN), a Jurassic sauropod from Tanzania, Africa, and with a name meaning "gigantic giraffe," is thought to have had a 33-foot-long neck. A giraffe, the longest animal alive today, measures a mere 18 feet from top to toe.

● Most mammals have the same number of neck bones. If they are long-necked, they simply have longer bones. But fossils show long-necked dinosaurs had more neck bones than others.

No one is sure, however, about the way *Tanystropheus* held its head. Some scientists suggest it may have rested its neck on the ground when it came onto land; but if so, its neck must have been a dreadful hindrance to movement. Others think it may have held its neck in an S-shape, much like a swan, only extending it to its full length when feeding from the water.

But the longest-necked creatures ever to populate the oceans were the plesiosaurs, prehistoric marine reptiles that existed for more than 100 million years. Although they lived mostly in the water, they were able to drag themselves onto the shore to lay their eggs, no easy task for such large creatures since their barrel-shaped bodies would have been a dead weight on land. *Muraeonosaurus* (<u>MOOR</u>-EYE-ON-OH-<u>SOR</u>-US), a typical plesiosaur, could swim underwater using four powerful flippers. Its long neck was also useful because it needed to come up every now and then to fill its lungs with air.

One of the great mysteries yet to be solved by paleontologists is why such long-necked, enormous creatures all died out. Nature does not continue with failures. So perhaps reptiles and other animals, too, now exist at the optimum size for survival. After all, if reptiles with longer and longer necks had continued to evolve, chances are their legs and torsos would have toppled over or collapsed under the strain.

29

TALES OF TOADS

The tiny black toad known scientifically as *Bufo exsul* (<u>BOOF</u>-OH <u>EX</u>-SOOL) is only found in an area close to Death Valley, California. No one is sure how many currently exist; but they are known to have become endangered because their tadpoles frequently dried up due to lack of water. Other toads, meanwhile, are rare for different reasons.

The midwife toads were given this name because of the exceptional way in which the males look after the eggs and attend them until they hatch out into tadpoles, in much the same way as a human midwife (a type of nurse specializing in maternity care) will help a human mother give birth to her baby.

The midwife toad from the Spanish island of Majorca was first discovered as recently as 1977, but as a fossil instead of a live species. This gave scientists the impression that it was probably extinct. Three years later, however, a living, breathing specimen of *Alytes muletensis* (AL-<u>EYE</u>-TEEZ MOOL-ET-<u>EN</u>-SIS), as this species of midwife toad is known, was discovered on this Mediterranean island.

HIDDEN HABITAT
Predators are not a problem because the Majorcan midwife toad rarely sees the light of day, hiding itself away in the crevices of the island's steep coastal cliffs.

COLOR CODED
Golden toads of Costa Rica provide an excellent example of sexually dimorphic (different) amphibians. The males, as in the photograph *above,* are all a golden orange; but the females, smaller in size, are black with yellow-edged scarlet blotches.

The Majorcan midwife toad had previously escaped notice because its favorite habitat lay deep within the very steep limestone cliffs that line the island's coast.

LOST GOLD

You would find it difficult, too, to locate specimens of the golden toad. These amphibians not only inhabit a very restricted area of cloud forest in Costa Rica, Central America, but have also gone into severe decline due to any or a combination of several possible causes. First, the males seem to outnumber the females by 8 to 1, so that there is tremendous competition among the males for a mate.

The breeding season of the golden toad is also very short and occurs only between April and June. Climatic conditions at that time can have a marked effect. If, for instance, too much rainfall occurs, the eggs can easily be washed away and fail to survive.

If, on the other hand, there is too little rainfall, the eggs may simply dry up and not be viable.

Curiously, the golden frog of Panama, also in Central America, known scientifically as *Atelopus varius zeteki* (AT-EL-OH-PUS VA-REE-US ZET-EK-EE), is also endangered. Its habitat is a 2-mile-wide valley almost entirely surrounded by mountains, but the area has been turned into a resort. At first, it was a major attraction to tourists to watch the cute golden frogs as they hopped around or sat on rocks by streams, basking in the sun. Visitors even collected them to take home as souvenirs, so that they have now virtually disappeared from the region.

The Puerto Rican crested toad is now also thought to be almost extinct, surviving only in small numbers on the northwest and southwest coasts of the island due mainly to drainage of its breeding sites, land development, and predation by birds.

This species (in which the females are larger than the males and have rougher skin and a higher crest above the eyes) does not breed at regular intervals, but seems to wait for ideal climatic conditions. This sometimes means a gap of a year or more between generations. There is now a captive breeding program for the Puerto Rican crested toad, however, and conservationists are working to preserve its natural habitat in case it can be reintroduced into the wild. Meanwhile, this very elusive crested toad has been officially listed as a threatened species by the United States Fish and Wildlife Service.

Lost Tortoises

From fossil evidence scientists know the shell of *Meiolania* (<u>MEYE</u>-OL-<u>AHN</u>-EE-AH), depicted *below* in the illustration of one of these giant tortoises following another, was up to 4 feet in length. Other tortoises, too, have reached massive proportions.

Tortoises and turtles first appeared about 200 million years ago, and the largest ever to have lived was a 13-foot-long sea creature known as *Archelon* (<u>ARK</u>-EL-ON), which existed over 65 million years ago toward the end of the reign of the dinosaurs.

Meiolania, which dates from Pleistocene times, had a horned skull, and it alone measured about 2 feet across. However, the horns, although magnificent in appearance, must have prevented this tortoise from withdrawing its head into its shell. Remains have been found on Lord Howe Island off the coast of New South Wales, Australia.

DELICIOUS FARE

Giant tortoises that have become extinct in more modern times include the giant tortoise of Mauritius, which has not been seen since 1700. It probably died out for the same reason as the Rodriguez giant tortoise, which lived on a nearby Indian Ocean island – that is, overhunting for its meat and shell. One person who tasted it said the flesh was so succulent that even when served plain, it seemed to be garnished with a rich sauce.

From the early 18th century onward until this tortoise became extinct about 100 years later, ships would even stop at the island of Rodriguez just to take on board as many of these creatures as they could pack into the holds of their vessels.

HORNY PROBLEM
The two horns adorning *Meiolania's* head probably made it impossible for this giant tortoise to retreat into its shell. This may have made it vulnerable to large, meat-eating predators.

ISLAND SPECIES

Some giant tortoises from the Galápagos Islands in the Pacific Ocean, where they were first discovered by Europeans in the 16th century, have also become extinct, even though the very name Galápagos is derived from a Spanish term meaning "a place where tortoises thrive." Here, once again, large numbers of the tortoises were killed for their meat from the 17th century onward. The Charles Island tortoise disappeared in 1876, for example, and the Barrington Island tortoise has not been seen since 1890.

Some are said to have measured more than 2 feet across their shells and may have weighed as much as 200 pounds. They must have been very hardy, too, because, when stowed on whaling ships and vessels of the United States Navy calling at the islands, some are reported to have survived merely on meager meals of prickly pear plants, while others got by for several months without any food or water at all and did not suffer any obvious ill effects.

The tortoises of the Galápagos Islands came in many different shapes. One saddlebacked species from Abingdon Island, for example, had a thin shell and a yellow face. But scientists think that they could interbreed.

The fate of one Galápagos tortoise seems not finally to have been decided, however. Once found on Abingdon Island, it disappeared due to hunting by visiting sailors and whalers. In 1972, however, there was a wonderful surprise. A live specimen and tracks were discovered. Some years later droppings were also found, and analysis showed they were only a few years old. So perhaps other supposedly extinct turtles lurk elsewhere in the world and are yet to be rediscovered.

Fact file

- How the tortoise *Meiolania* got from Australia to the small South Pacific islands on which it lived remains a mystery because it could not swim.

- The shell of a tortoise is known as its carapace (KA-RAH-PAYS). They differ a lot in size and shape, as well as color and markings.

- In the 18th century some of the giant tortoises of Mauritius disappeared because their eggs and their young were eaten by pigs. All had become extinct by 1760.

- Some giant tortoises were ground-feeders; others fed on the lower leaves of trees and shrubs.

MORE LOST TESTUDINATES

Once symbols of good health and general well-being, and often living for more than a century, ironically many species of turtles and tortoises have now either disappeared altogether or have gone into very serious decline.

One of the rarest of all the testudinates is the so-called bog turtle. Tiny in size, it has been described as a gem of a creature. Indeed, because it was so appealing to collectors, and now its swampy habitat has been drained, this water tortoise has virtually vanished in the eastern United States.

END USES
Not only is the flesh of testudinates (turtles and tortoises) sometimes eaten, their shells are also prized and put to many uses, as the musical instrument in the photograph *below* clearly shows.

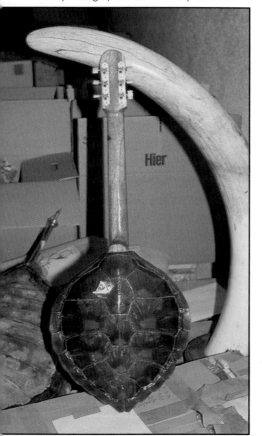

Hier

Among the true tortoises native to North America and protected by law are the Texas tortoise and the desert tortoise, both of which were once threatened by the pet trade. The Mexican gopher tortoise, meanwhile, is extinct in some parts of this region and in other parts is still hunted for food by locals.

Green turtles are now very rare, too, and said to be the most valuable reptile in the world. In spite of their name, they vary in color a lot, and their shells range from black to brown, gray and, of course, green. They are the largest of all marine turtles; and in the attempt to improve their endangered status, scientists often attach radio transmitters to their backs so they can track their movements.

ILLEGAL TRADE
In some parts of the world there are laws protecting turtles and tortoises; but as shown in the display *below*, such legislation is often ignored by poachers.

They excel at swimming, and those making their nests on Ascension Island have even been known to swim all the way to the Brazilian coast to find suitable feeding grounds.

When mature, the green turtle may weigh as much as 330 pounds and extend to over 3 feet in length. But the babies are tiny, and you could even hold one in the palm of your hand. After hatching on the beach, they make the journey to the ocean at night but still risk being eaten by all sorts of predators on the way, so that few ever survive to adulthood.

Strangely, those eggs that are incubated below a certain temperature always hatch into males; so cooler temperatures in the region of Ascension Island may have something to do with their demise since there may be fewer females born to produce a new generation.

Scientists have also found that many adult green turtles, although they have lived perfectly healthily since they first came into existence millions of years ago, now tend to develop nasty tumors that decrease their population even further. According to one theory, they may be due to swimming in polluted waters.

A SAD DEMISE
The last two giant saddleback tortoises on the island of Rodriguez were spotted trapped down a ravine, as shown *right*, in 1795.

THE REAL ESTATE THREAT

The loggerhead turtle in the photograph *below* is no longer found in great numbers along the Atlantic coast of the United States since It cannot come ashore to lay its eggs due to the building of houses close to the beaches.

Fact file

● Land-dwelling turtles, although sometimes seeking out marshy ponds, are usually known as tortoises. True turtles prefer the salty ocean.

● The construction of coastal resorts has destroyed the natural habitat of some species of turtles, so that they have drastically declined in numbers in the cause of commerce.

● Some governments have now created turtle reserves, ban hunting turtles within national waters, and prohibit the sale of their shells and flesh in the attempt to save these testudinates from extinction.

● Turtles have to crawl onto land to lay their eggs, which are frequently taken to be hatched by poachers, who usually also try to capture the mother.

LOST LIZARDS

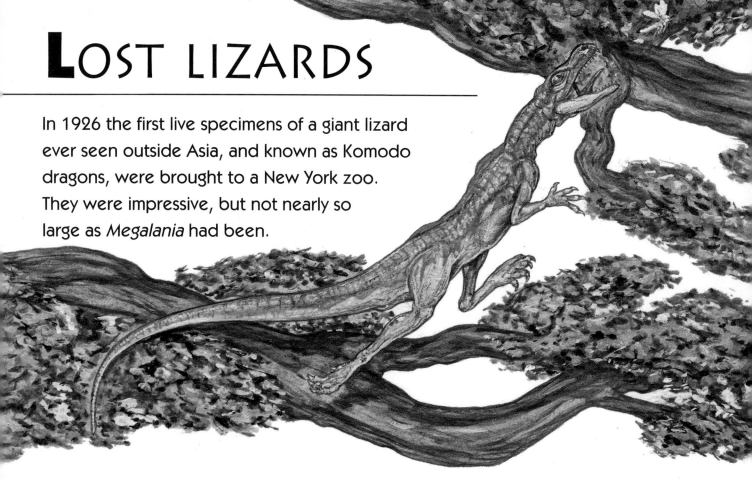

In 1926 the first live specimens of a giant lizard ever seen outside Asia, and known as Komodo dragons, were brought to a New York zoo. They were impressive, but not nearly so large as *Megalania* had been.

Thought to have been an ancestor of the Komodo dragon, *Megalania* – a giant monitor lizard from what is now Australia – was enormous. In fact, it may have extended to 20 feet in length. Fossils have been dated to show it must have lived at the same time as some of our own early ancestors. No wonder, then, so many legends grew up around it! But no one knows why it died out.

We can only guess it may have been exterminated by humans who found it horrific because of its size. Indeed, like the fictional heroes who went dragon-slaying, anyone killing a *Megalania* may have been praised for eliminating what was regarded as a fearful beast.

Whatever the truth, the largest monitor lizard to be found in Australia today grows to just 6 feet in length and has the scientific name *Varanus giganteus* (VA-<u>RAHN</u>-US JEYE-<u>GANT</u>-EE-US.).

DOTTED DAY GECKO
The colorful Rodriguez day gecko, which had a blue spotted green body and yellow neck, and which once lived on an island near Mauritius, became extinct around 1920 due to destruction of its natural habitat and attack by rats and cats.

DARTING THROUGH THE TREETOPS
One of the earliest reptiles to evolve and looking very much like a modern lizard, *Hylonomus* (<u>HEYE</u>-LOH-<u>NOH</u>-MUS), *above*, was a Carboniferous forest-dweller.

Other lizards have become extinct more recently for a variety of different reasons. Some from the West Indies, for example, became the prey of the mongoose and of cats, rats, and birds.

A number have disappeared, meanwhile, because they were hunted purely for sport; and one particular species of lizard, from a tiny island near Guadeloupe in the West Indies, vanished after its natural habitat was destroyed in a terrible hurricane. There are times, too, when building work can affect a reptile population. This is what happened on Ratas Island in the Mediterranean, for example.

Many skinks, a type of long-bodied lizard most commonly found in tropical Asia and Africa, have also either disappeared completely or become rare over the centuries due primarily to droughts and subsequent loss of vegetation. This undoubtedly contributed to the demise of a giant skink, almost 24 inches long and once found on the Cape Verde Islands in the Atlantic Ocean, for instance. Convicts, banished there in 1833 during a terrible famine, were forced to turn any surviving lizards into part of their staple diet, so that numbers must have dwindled very rapidly after that. It finally disappeared about one hundred years later.

The 20-inch-long giant skink from Mauritius, one of the Mascarenes, a group of islands lying off the east coast of Africa, has not been seen since the end of the 17th century. Like that curious, flightless bird the dodo, which was also native to some of these Indian Ocean islands, large numbers of this skink may have fallen victim to pigs and rats.

Later, toward the end of the 19th century, a 6-inch-long, tongue-flicking, striped skink from nearby Réunion also became extinct.

Observers of the time noticed it was very tame, a factor that undoubtedly made it vulnerable to predatory mongooses and rats.

On another island of the same group lizards known as the day and night varieties of the Rodriguez gecko also once lived. The small day gecko vanished in the early 20th century in spite of its ability to change color as a form of camouflage. The far larger night gecko, not seen since the mid-19th century, was as long as your arm and bold enough to feed on tiny mammals and birds' eggs.

DYING BREEDS

But what of those species of lizards that are listed as endangered today? Among them is the blunt-nosed leopard lizard of California, whose former natural arid habitat has now been irrigated to provide land for farming, an environment to which the lizard is entirely unsuited. The San Diego horned lizard, so called because of all its skin projections, has also become disturbingly rare in southern California, as has the black legless lizard, which strangely, as you might guess from its name, has no limbs at all.

LONG GONE
Megalania prisca, below, a survivor until prehistoric times, when it was probably hunted by early humans, was almost twice as long as the average car.

RHYNCHOSAURS

A new species of the tuatara (<u>TOO</u>-AH-<u>TAH</u>-RAH) of New Zealand, a very odd-looking reptile, was discovered as recently as 1989. But did you know these creatures had a remarkable ancestor back in Triassic times, when dinosaurs had just started to evolve?

A distant relative of its ancestors, the rhynchosaurs (<u>RIN</u>-KOH-<u>SORS</u>), the tuatara is known as a "living fossil" because it has changed so little since ancient times. Like the tuataras, the rhynchosaurs are classed as diapsid reptiles, which means they had two holes in the back of their skulls just behind their eye sockets. Powerful muscles extended from these holes to their jaws, so that their mouths could be opened wide.

Rhynchosaurs may also have looked like some species of dinosaurs but they belonged to an entirely different family of Triassic reptiles. Their remains have been found all over the world. Resembling giant pigs, they grew to be about six feet in length and fed mostly on tough seed ferns, cracking into them with their beaked mouths. At the end of Triassic times, however, they vanished completely in a mass extinction. Today, their relative, the tuatara, shown *below*, has so far managed to escape being wiped out but is extremely rare. It looks very much like a lizard, as you can see, but there are some important differences.

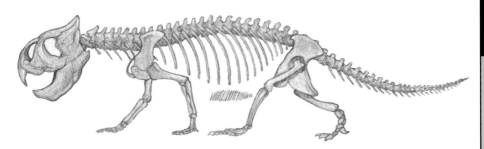

TRIASSIC REMAINS

Remains show a rhynchosaur had a barrel-shaped body and large guts to help it digest all the plants it ate. It also had a big, beaklike mouth; and some species, such as *Hyperodapedon* (<u>HEYE</u>-PER-OH-DAH-<u>PEE</u>-DON), *above*, had tusklike bones on its head.

For instance, it has a mysterious third eye, which is covered in scales, and two sets of teeth in its upper mouth.

The tuatara (its name means "old spiny back" in the language of the Maoris) is a nocturnal creature, coming out at night to catch and eat both insects and small lizards.

Two species are now known; but so few remain in the wild that extinction or, at the very least, classification as an endangered creature is likely.

The main reason for this decline is that the introduction of rats, wild cats, and pigs into New Zealand caused tuataras to become hunted by these active predators. As a result, most are now kept in captivity in a valiant attempt to preserve the species.

Numbers continue to dwindle, however, because a female tuatara only lays eggs once every four years. These eggs then take another whole year to hatch. Tuataras reach adulthood at the age of 13 and have been known to live for up to 50 years after that.

Fact file

- A tuatara can grow up to nine inches in length, and the adults weigh little more than one pound.

- Other examples of living fossils include the coelacanth fish and the horseshoe crab, both of which have changed very little since prehistoric times.

- There are two classes of diapsids. The so-called lower group includes the tuatara, snakes, lizards, and iguanas; the higher group, dinosaurs, crocodiles, and birds.

- Rhynchosaurs became extinct about 215 million years ago.

- Remains of rhynchosaurs have been found in many parts of the world such as North America, Brazil, Argentina, Tanzania, Germany, and Great Britain.

SOLE SURVIVOR

The tuatara is the only survivor of the ancient reptile group known colloquially as the beak-heads. This group is even older then the dinosaurs, having first appeared 220 million years ago. It now only lives on small islands off New Zealand.

SEYMOURIA

This strange creature has been the subject of much debate among scientists, who are divided over whether to class *Seymouria* (SEE-<u>MOR</u>-EE-AH) as an amphibian or a reptile. Read on and decide for yourself how *you* would classify it.

In 1917 the skeletal remains of an intriguing prehistoric creature that was subsequently named *Seymouria* were unearthed in an area not far from the town of Seymour in Texas. It was to prove to be a most unusual species.

GROOVY THEORY
From grooves in the skulls of a young *Seymouria*, whose remains are shown *above*, paleontologists think it could hear well even in the water.

VITAL STATISTICS
The fossilized bones showed that *Seymouria* had four legs, a sturdy body, and a short tail. It measured about two feet in length, and its skin had probably been scaly although, as with most other fossil finds, only *Seymouria's* bones have been preserved. A small head, meanwhile, indicated it would have had a small brain and was therefore almost certainly of very limited intelligence.

Seymouria may not have been very fast on the ground, so that it was vulnerable to attack. Nevertheless, it had plenty of sharp teeth with which to fight off intrepid predators. Its diet would have comprised insects and any other small creatures it came across on land or in the water. Chances are it also fed on the leftovers of any dead animals killed by far larger predators.

Some scientists regard *Seymouria* as the most advanced of all early amphibians. But it also had much in common with a reptile. For example, the long bones in *Seymouria's* feet are very much like those of both prehistoric and present-day reptiles.

IN PERMIAN TIMES
Seymouria lived among lowlands and damp, swampy areas. Predatory pelycosaurs such as *Varanosaurus* may have found *Seymouria* a tasty snack.

STANDING ALONE

Yet it also differed from most of the amphibians. Its skull structure had fewer bones, while its jaw was much shorter. But unlike true reptiles, *Seymouria* probably laid its eggs in water, demonstrating there must once have been some sort of link between amphibians and reptiles.

However, *Seymouria* seems to have been the end of an evolutionary line rather than the start of something new. Indeed, according to another school of thought, *Seymouria*, which lived about 280 million years ago in Permian times, when amphibians were on the decline, must have been descended from a completely different line of animals, which, so far, paleontologists have not clearly identified.

Reptiles owe much of their success to the fact that they lay eggs with hard shells, which gives them a better chance of survival. Amphibians, on the other hand, might dehydrate or die if they spend too much time on land and need to stay near water to lay their eggs. If, therefore, it was partly an amphibian and partly a reptile, *Seymouria* would have had the best of both worlds.

It seems reasonable to draw the conclusion that *Seymouria* lived in the water when young even if not aquatic as adults. The fossilized skulls of juveniles bear this out and show a system of grooves, indicating these creatures were capable of detecting sound waves underwater.

Fact file

- Reptiles first appeared on Earth during Carboniferous times. They adapted to living on dry land and ruled the planet for 200 million years.

- Remains of *Seymouria* have been found in central Germany as well as in Texas, Utah, and New Mexico. The discovery of remains on different continents supports the theory that there was once a single supercontinent on our planet. Scientists call this land mass *Pangaea* (PAN-<u>JEE</u>-AH).

- *Diadectes* (DEYE-A-<u>DEKT</u>-EEZ), a relative of *Seymouria,* was a 6-foot-long plant-eater and one of an evolutionary line of reptiles, including dinosaurs, that eventually led to the development of the first birds.

EXTINCT FROGS

Over recent decades scientists have noticed that in various parts of the world some species of frogs appear to be declining in number or are becoming deformed. Others seem to have disappeared altogether. Why is this happening?

The Palestinian painted frog was first identified as a species as recently as 1940. But within just 16 years it became extinct. About 3.25 inches long when mature, it was first identified

SWAMP-LOVER
The Palestinian painted frog *below* was used to swampy conditions but died out when land north of Lake Tiberias on the Israeli border was drained as part of a land-reclamation plan.

from two mature specimens and two tadpoles. Strangely, it is the only painted frog to have been found living east of the Mediterranean Sea. It also differed from other known types of painted frogs in a few additional ways. Its front legs were longer, and it had very distinctive markings.

There were red-and-white blotches, as well as spotted areas, on its 3.5-inch-long, rust-colored body, and it had gray underparts.

It must have been very disappointing for the person who found the first two frogs because it turned out one of them at least had cannibalistic tendencies!

The bigger of the two frogs, which was a female, must have become extremely hungry or disturbed in some way because she suddenly gobbled down the other one. There seems to be no surviving record of what happened to the two tadpoles that had been found at the same time, however.

In 1955 one further specimen was discovered, and from the large size of this female it was noticed that the two previous frogs must have been juveniles. No further specimen of a Palestinian painted frog, depicted in the illustration *below left*, has come to light since that date.

TAKING A GAMBLE

Another species of frog that has become extinct is one that lived in the region of Las Vegas, the gambling capital of the United States. Known as the Vegas Valley leopard frog, it became rare after natural springs in the area were diverted. But that was not the only factor. When trout were introduced to the area, these fish ate the frogs' eggs and tadpoles, with the result that the last time this frog was seen was back in 1942.

Sometimes, too, frogs have disappeared because people find them cute and like to collect them. Viruses are also known to kill frogs. In Great Britain, for example, disease carried by goldfish and bullfrogs imported from the United States is taking its toll.

Other reasons why some frogs have become scarce could well include the liking some people have for eating frogs' legs and the use of pesticides. In 1997 the Australian government even banned use of some herbicides near water.

There have been reports, too, that fungicides can take their toll on frogs. In Minnesota, for instance, it was shown they could stunt tadpole growth and affect the normal sexual development of frogs. The pollution of watercourses with detergents, meanwhile, has sometimes prevented frogs from breathing through their skin. Parasites, such as the trematodes, can also sometimes be to blame for the decline of some species of frog.

Frogs first appeared more than 200 million years ago in Triassic times, at the time of the early dinosaurs. These amphibians were under 4 inches long even when fully

Fact file

- Land reclamation is meant for the good; but when swamps were drained on the Israeli-Syrian border, it led to loss of the Palestinian painted frog's natural habitat.

- A collector who looked after a single specimen of the Palestinian painted frog found that it was active only at night.

- The scientific name for the Palestinian painted frog is *Discoglossus nigriventer* (DISK-OH-GLOS-US NIG-REE-VENT-ER.)

- One of the rarest frogs today is the Panamanian golden frog, which is found only in a three-square-mile area of Panama. Numbers have decreased because they were once exported, and tourists were frequently tempted to acquire them as pets.

ONE OF THE FIRST
Found in Madagascar, off the east coast of Africa, the species of frog known as *Triadobatrachus* (TRY-AD-OH-BAT-RAHK-US), *above left*, is thought to have been among the first to evolve.

grown and are thought by scientists to have evolved from creatures known as *Temnospondyls* (TEM-NOH-SPOND-ILS), which also had tadpole young.

43

ON THE BRINK

Crocodiles, lizards, and snakes are still widely killed for their skins because some governments have been slow to introduce legislation to spare these creatures. This is just one of the reasons why so many species of reptiles, and amphibians, too, continue to dwindle.

When, in the 19th century, naturalist Charles Darwin visited the Galápagos Islands, he found so many land iguana burrows on just one of the group of islands that he had to tread very carefully to avoid them. Today, however, there are only a few of these creatures to be found throughout the archipelago.

All wildlife on the Galápagos Islands is now protected by law, however, so conservationists hope that before too long their numbers may start to increase.

One species of caiman is also legally protected in Brazil. However, poaching continues because of the high price its skin will fetch and the fact that only a minimal fine is ever imposed by the law-enforcement agencies. For some unexplainable reason, meanwhile, other species of caiman are not protected by law.

In any event, few officials can tell one species of caiman from another.

International trade in the Indian whipsnake also continues, despite an export ban. Elsewhere, too, campaigns for the preservation of certain endangered species have yet to prove effective. The hawksbill turtle, once common in all the world's warm oceans, is now increasingly rare, for example, as a result of continued demand from the jewelry trade and, in turn, the public for items made from its shell.

Western collectors also seek specimens of the exquisite radiated tortoise from the island of Madagascar, off the east coast of Africa, even though the locals believe they have supernatural powers and that it is unlucky even to touch them.

From time to time, too, endangered and protected species of Indonesian turtles are smuggled abroad and suddenly turn up in private hands elsewhere in the world.

SOLE SURVIVOR
The marine iguana, *left,* the only present-day lizard with an aquatic habitat and as such a throwback to prehistoric times, is only to be found on the Galápagos Islands off Ecuador, South America.

A DARK FUTURE?
The spectacled caiman of South America, so-called because of ridges surrounding its eager eyes that make it appear to be wearing glasses, is fast being wiped out by hunters after its hide.

BRED TO EXTINCTION

Another reason why some creatures become severely endangered is that they inbreed to such an extent that a number become malformed and have both male and female sexual organs. A viper from a tiny island off Brazil, South America, is a prime example. Here, this highly venomous and arboreal snake could find very little by way of prey and would have been at risk of extinction for this reason alone if it had not been able to rely on catching birds when they flew into the trees.

At the beginning of the 20th century there were thousands of these vipers on the island. However, by the 1950s comparatively few specimens remained, and only about three in every one hundred were female, while the majority of the rest showed both male and female characteristics.

These vipers failed to reproduce and rapidly declined. Zoologists hoped to find a few captive specimens or some of the same species on nearby islands, but without success, so that none exists today. Isolated, inbreeding species inevitably die out, and so conservationists continually strive to avoid such a calamity.

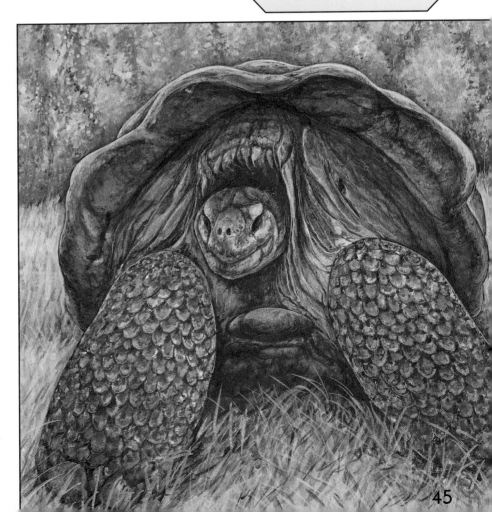

PROTECTED SPECIES
The rookery (breeding site) of the giant tortoise, *right*, one of the few surviving on the Galápagos Islands, is now protected by both Ecuador and a branch of the United Nations.

GLOSSARY

amphibians
a group of cold-blooded creatures, usually living on land but breeding in water, such as frogs and toads

aquatic
living in water

arboreal
living in or among trees

archipelago
a group of islands

bipedal
walking on two limbs

caiman
a tropical crocodilian

camouflage
a disguise achieved by blending into the environment

cannibalistic
eating its own kind

Carboniferous times
a period lasting from about 345 to 280 million years ago

Cretaceous times
a period lasting from about 144 to 65 million years ago

crocodilian
one of the crocodile family

detergent
a cleansing chemical substance

drought
lack of rainfall

ectothermic
cold-blooded

endothermic
warm-blooded

fungicide
a substance that kills a harmful fungus

herbicide
a substance that kills weeds

herpetologist
someone who studies reptiles

Jurassic times
a period lasting from about 213 to 144 million years ago

Mesozoic times
an era covering Triassic, Jurassic, and Cretaceous times

nodule
a small knob, lump, or swelling

parasite
any animal or plant living off another from which it obtains nourishment

pesticide
a substance that kills pests such as destructive insects

quarry
prey chased by a predator

reptiles
a group of egg-laying, cold-blooded creatures characterized by lungs and a covering of scales or plates, such as tortoises, snakes, crocodiles, and lizards

sauropods
a group name for many Jurassic long-necked, plant-eating dinosaurs

semiaquatic
living some of the time in water

tadpole
the stage before a fully grown frog or toad

theropods
a predatory group of dinosaurs, mostly bipedal

trematode
a type of prehistoric flatworm

testudinate
general term used to describe turtles and tortoises

throwback
an animal or plant with the characteristics of an earlier or more primitive species

Triassic times
a period lasting from about 249 to 213 million years ago

vertebra (*pl.* vertebrae)
one of the segments of the backbone

virus
a disease-spreading organism

48